TEACHING CHILDREN ABOUT PRAYER

by Judy Gattis Smith

TEACHING CHILDREN ABOUT PRAYER

ISBN 0-940754-56-8

EDUCATIONAL MINISTRIES, INC.

CONTENTS

INTRODUCTION..5

Session One...7
ATTITUDES

Session Two...11
HOW DO WE APPROACH GOD?

Session Three...15
PRAYERS OF ADORATION

Session Four...19
CONFESSION AND THANKSGIVING

Session Five...23
PRAYERS OF SUPPLICATION

INTRODUCTION

We want to foster spiritual growth in our children. One of the ways we want our youngsters to grow spiritually is through prayer. It has been my experience in church school teaching that the hardest lesson we have to teach children is how to pray.

For one thing, prayer is always God-initiated. First our hearts are stirred to long for God and seek God in prayer.

But there is still the responsibility of the teacher to create the setting where this can take place and to help children understand the many dimensions of prayer.

Prayer is an important lesson in the Christian faith that can best be taught by experiencing it. But how and where do we begin?

Ideally prayer would evolve through the church school with children at each age level growing and developing in their ability to experience God and to feel comfortable communicating with God.

The truth and the challenge, however, is that we do not often find this ideal.

This was my experience when I taught a group of elementary grade boys and girls about prayer.

Let me share with you the plans we developed and the goals we were seeking to obtain, for the purpose of giving you something concrete to use in teaching your elementary children about prayer. I will include the reactions and responses of my particular class. Though yours will be different, perhaps we can find a common strand.

The sessions were held on Sunday mornings during the regular one-hour church school period for five weeks.

SESSION ONE:

ATTITUDES

We first attempted to find out the attitude of the class toward God and prayer. Systems, techniques, words to use or to kneel, sit or stand, these things, we decided, would come second.

Step 1. We began by looking at what prayer means to these children.

First, they filled out the questionnaire at the end of this session (on page 10).

PRAYER QUESTIONNAIRE

I. When do you pray?   Often   Sometimes   Seldom   Never
1. at bedtime
2. before meals
3. when in danger
4. when afraid
5. when happy
6. when thankful
7. when lonely
8. when wanting something
9. when seeing something beautiful
10. when you have done wrong
11. when you want to be forgiven

12. before a test
13. before a sports event
14. after a test

II. How often do you pray?
   daily   once a week   only in emergencies   never

III. Why do you pray or why don't you pray?

One student said: "*I'm not going to sit in a room and talk to somebody who doesn't talk back.*" (God is seen as aloof, silent and withdrawn.) But another child replied, "*I pray because I love God and I love to pray.*"

IV. Complete the sentence: Prayer is _____

One student said: "*...very boring. Especially the long preacher's prayer in church.*" (Prayer is seen as impersonal, dreary, institutional.) But another child said, "*...something nice.*"

These questionnaires were not signed or discussed at this point. They were turned in to the teacher. The object was to begin to focus the class' thinking and to give the teacher some realistic background from which to proceed.

Step 2: Children were given paper and crayons and told to draw anything they wished with no other explanation or instruction.

Step 3: Children were given a chance to show and explain their pictures.

Step 4: Teacher input. Here are some quotations. Listen and see if you agree:

"Tell me what you pay attention to and I will tell you who you are."

"As a person thinketh in his heart, so is he."

What do you think these quotes mean? (Accept answers from the class.)

Class, we want to develop a frame of mind in which all of our lives focus on God. As Christians our main concern is to live lives in complete obedience before God. Think about the things that really interest you and just try to bring these things before God. How do they fit in with God's unique plan for your life?

Step 5: Children pick a picture from a magazine of something they'd really like to have. (My class picked very material things — big cars, big homes, motorcycles, jewels.)

We went around the circle of class members. The children showed the pictures of their desired object and then the teacher made a response such as these: "You may have this object but only if you'd have to feel sick every day of your life. Do you still want it?"

"You may have this object but only if you will cut off your leg in exchange for it. Do you still want it?"

"You may have this object but only if you'll always live alone with no family to share with. Do you still want it?"

"You may have this but only on the understanding that you drop dead immediately."

The point of this exercise was to use exaggeration to shock the children into considering what was really important in their lives. In every incident in our class, the child did not want the object.

Teacher: Here is an assignment for the week. As you go through the day, stop and check what you are thinking about. God wants you to have and enjoy good things. Things were created for pleasure but things are not God. Is your life centering on things that are ultimately important? God is the reason and the fulfillment of your existence.

A final thought on prayer: Before you think of praying, God is thinking of you. Before you awoke this morning, God was awake and calling you. Long after you fall asleep this night, God will watch over you. God seeks you. Why pray? Because we must take this God seriously.

Needed for Session One:
1. copies of questionnaire for all children (see below)
2. pencils
3. paper and crayons for a drawing for each child
4. current magazines. Choose ones with lots of advertisements
5. scissors

Session One Outline:
1. Fill out questionnaire
2. Spontaneous drawing and discussion of drawings
3. "My desire" pictures and discussion

PRAYER QUESTIONNAIRE

I. When do you pray?   Often   Sometimes   Seldom   Never
1. at bedtime
2. before meals
3. when in danger
4. when afraid
5. when happy
6. when thankful
7. when lonely
8. when you want something
9. when you see something beautiful
10. when you have done wrong
11. when you want to be forgiven
12. before a test
13. before a sports event
14. after a test

II. How often do you pray?

    Daily   once a week   only in emergencies   never

III. Why do you pray or why don't you pray?

_____

_____

IV. Complete this sentence: Prayer is _____

_____

_____

SESSION TWO:

HOW DO WE APPROACH GOD?

Objective: To get children started simply with praying.

Step 1: Ask the class to come up with as many names for God as they can. List on the board all these names. Class usually comes up with "Father." Ask, "What about Mother?" Though female language has been a concern in theological circles for several years, I found it to be a shocking idea in three different local elementary grade church school settings. "No!," "God can't be Mother," "Isn't God a man?" Teacher replied, "Well, *is* God a man?" "No! But God certainly isn't a woman!" In all of these settings, two urban and one rural, the response was heated and strongly responded to.

After listing some names for God, ask each member of your class to choose the name they felt most comfortable with in addressing God and write it on a slip of paper. (In my particular class, every child chose the word "God" though we listed a dozen names and discussed them.)

Step 2: Now imagine God is right in front of you. You have called God by the name you feel most comfortable with. Imagine God now addressing you by name and asking you, "*Sarah*, what do you want?"

11

Write in a simple sentence what you would say. These prayers were turned in to the teacher unsigned.

Here are some of the responses of my class:

"God, I want to have fun playing football today and have a fair game."

"God, give me a good day."

"God, I want my grandfather's arthrstest to go away."

"God, I want to have time today to clean up my room and to have time to play."

"God, I would like for me and Melissa not to fight."

Step 3: Role-play

Children come together in a semi-circle. On a slip of paper, a prayer is described. A child draws a slip, reads the paper, and then acts it out for the whole group.

Situations:

1. You've gotten a bad grade on your report card. You pray to God to give you strength to be honest with your parents.

2. You want a bike for Christmas. You tell God you've earned it and deserve it.

3. You have a math test tomorrow. You pray that your math teacher will get sick so you won't have to take the test.

4. You are always fighting with your little brother. You pray for ways to be more understanding.

5. Your neighbor's puppy was run over. You pray that she will get a new puppy.

6. There is a kid in school that everybody picks on. You pray for ways to be his friend and to stand up to the rest of the children.

Following each role-play, the class discusses the content and approach of each prayer. Discuss what prayers could be improved. How?

This was a helpful activity for me as teacher in learning where my class was in their feelings about prayer and helpful for the students I think in opening up new ways of praying for them.

For example, in No. 5, the class thought at first that praying for a new puppy was the most helpful prayer for the neighbor. As they discussed it, prayers for the neighbor surfaced.

Needed for Session Two:
1. paper and pencil for each student
2. role-play situations written out

Session Two Outline:
1. List names for God and discuss.
2. Write a simple prayer.
3. Role-play prayer examples and discuss.

SESSION THREE:

PRAYERS OF ADORATION

Introduce the class to different types of prayers that are a part of the Christian tradition. Use this familiar pattern:

A Adoration
C Confession
T Thanksgiving
S Supplication

Step 1: Introduce the four types of prayer. Students look up biblical examples of each. Class reads these together. Some in unison, some with a solo reader.

Adoration — Psalm 95:1-7
Confession — Psalm 32:1-7
Thanksgiving — Psalm 100
Supplication — Psalm 70:1-3, 5

Step 2: Today we will focus on prayers of adoration. To adore means to love greatly, to greatly respect.

In small discussion groups ask each student to share the most awesome event they have ever had or the most awesome thing they have ever seen. (In my small group discussions with elementary children, I have better discussions when I put boys together into a group and girls together into a group.)

In these small group discussions, some children mentioned storms they had been in, scenes of nature such as mountains and oceans. I was surprised to discover that many mentioned man-made things such as sky-scrapers and very large ships.

All answers are accepted without criticizing comments, and listed. These sheets from the small groups are put up around the room and read aloud when the whole group gathers again.

Teacher's summary: We pray prayers of adoration when we are aware of God's utter majesty, holiness and goodness. When we become aware of overwhelming power, see great beauty or an act of great goodness, we pray prayers of adoration.

Step 3: Give each child a piece of clay. On the record player use a magnificent arrangement of the *Doxology* for organ and choir. "Praise God from whom all blessings flow. Praise Him all creatures here below. Praise Him above ye heavenly host. Praise Father, Son and Holy Ghost" or similar awesome music. With this as background, children are to make something with the clay that shows the wonders of creation. Have the children share their creations. (The typical animals and plants were created but again I was surprised that two boys created large bombs. Before I could catch myself I commented, "Oh, you were supposed to show something God created." One of the boys replied, "It's a great wonder and God gave us minds to think of it.")

Step 4: On the board, list the following names for God:
Almighty God
Supreme Being
Creator God
All-Powerful God
All-Wise God
All-Loving God
All-Holy God

As in the previous week, the children are asked to pick one of these names they feel comfortable calling God. They write this on a slip of paper. Then, imagining this God standing before them, they imagine this God calling them by name and asking, "*Todd, what do you want?*" They should respond with a written sentence: (Almighty God), I wonder_____.

Step 5: The prayers are written and unsigned and turned in.

(In my particular experience, only one child in the class seemed to get the point. She wrote, "Creator God, I wonder at the mystery of turning leaves." Most of the prayers were of the calibre, "O Almighty God, I wonder if the Redskins will win.")

At the end of this session, I was struck with the difficulty of teaching wonder and awe to modern children. There is much that is awesome that is man-made today. God seems to have shrunk. How can we teach that all our man-made wonders, as overwhelming and powerful as they are, are but the tip of the iceberg to the majesty and wonder and awe of God? We say, as we marvel at the discoveries and inventions of science, if man is so wonderful, how much more wonderful must God the creator be?

Step 6: In a closing circle, have children sit quietly as teacher reads: "We bow before God's infinite majesty and holiness, trembling with awe at God's unapproachable might and radiance, before which angels and archangels veil their sight. Holy, holy, holy, Lord, God of Ghost. Heaven and earth are full of Thy glory."

Needed for Session Three:
1. Bibles
2. clay
3. record of adoration hymn
4. paper and pencil for each child

Session Three Outline:
1. Short Bible readings of four kinds of prayers
2. Small group work.
3. Create with clay.
4. Write prayers of adoration.

SESSION FOUR:

CONFESSION AND THANKSGIVING

After these three sessions of rather intense, mind-stretching activities and discussions, we felt a need for something more active, especially with our boys. So we chose to center this fourth session around active games.

Step 1: As students enter, a 5 x 7 card is pinned on their back. When all are assembled, give each a crayon and tell them they are going to play the game "Pig."

Step 2: The Game.

Instructions: Players form a line behind the leader. Each player tries to draw a picture of a pig on the card pinned on the back of the person directly in front. However, the leader keeps the line moving about the room, making it difficult for anyone to have much opportunity to draw! Winner is the sketch most nearly resembling a pig.

Step 3: After the game, read Luke 15:11-20 as the children stand around the table looking at the different pictures. Give special emphasis to verses 18 & 19a: "I will get up and go to my father and say, 'Father, I have sinned against God and against you. I am no longer fit to be called your son.'"

19

This is a prayer of confession. When we are down with the pigs and we realize what a mess we have made of everything, then we pray prayers of confession.

Share examples from class members of when they felt "down with the pigs." When have they felt separation and desperation?

Step 4: <u>Teacher:</u> The second kind of prayer we are looking at today is Prayers of Thanksgiving. Again, we will illustrate this type of prayer with a game.

Step 5: Game – Thanksgiving Rhythm

<u>Instructions:</u> Children sit in chairs in a circle. They clap this rhythmic pattern together: two slaps on their thighs, two claps, two snaps of fingers. The group practices until they all can do the rhythm together. Now they start around the circle, keeping the rhythm going but on the finger snaps, the person must say something he or she is thankful for.

<u>Two Rules:</u> You can't break the rhythm and you can't repeat a word that has already been said. If you break one of these rules, you are out. The game continues until only one player remains.

Step 6: Teacher reads Luke 17:11-19, The Ten Lepers

Step 7: Following the reading, the students go to tables and illustrate this story like a cartoon. They are given a long slip of paper divided into six sections. Using stick-figure characters, they put the story in cartoon form. Some may add words in bubbles for the characters' conversations. Cartoons were shared and posted around the room.

Needed for Session Four:
1. 5 x 7 cards with pins
2. crayons for each student
3. cartoon strip of paper for each student
4. pencils

Session Four Outline:
1. Play "Pig."
2. Read Prodigal Son.

3. Play thanksgiving rhythm.
4. Read Ten Lepers and illustrate in cartoon form.

SESSION FIVE:

PRAYERS OF SUPPLICATION

Step 1: Class is divided into two teams. Collect a number of pictures of Jesus praying from your file of church school pictures or magazines.

Step 2: Contest.

Teacher holds up one of the pictures. Group 1 looks at the picture, talks together about it, and then answers: What is this story of Jesus praying? If Group 1 does not know the answer, Group 2 is given the chance. Then Group 2 is shown the next picture and so on. The team that answers correctly is given a point.

We used these pictures:
Jesus' Baptism
Temptation in Wilderness
Calling the Disciples
Jesus Healing
In the Garden of Gethsemane
Transfiguration
Crucifixion
Jesus Teaching

Step 3: After the game discuss: Is it alright to ask God for things? Why does God not always give us what we ask for?

Teacher says: When prayer seems hazy and remote we can center on Jesus. We can look at all the times Jesus prayed and all the kinds of prayers he used. We have heard stories today of Jesus' solitary fasting and victory over temptation in the wilderness before he began his ministry. We heard the story of how Jesus prayed before he chose his 12 disciples. We heard about the terrible lonely prayer in Gethsemane just before the crucifixion. Jesus must have received great power from prayer. Isn't it interesting that the disciples who traveled with Jesus and were closest to him did not ask him how to *heal* (though they saw many examples of his healing). They did not ask him how to preach (though they listened to him). What they did ask was that he teach them to pray.

Step 4: Jesus answered them with what we now call the Lord's Prayer.

Use a large chart like this:

Our Father Who Art in Heaven
_____ Be Thy Name
Thy _____ _____
Thy _____ _____ _____
On_____ as it is in _____
Give us this day

_____ _____ _____
and forgive us our _____
as we forgive those who _____ _____ _____
And lead us not into _____
But deliver us from _____
For thine is the _____,
the _____
and the_____
forever and forever.
Amen.

Step 5: The class practices the Lord's Prayer until all in the class can say it.

Step 6: Class gathers around a worship table. Candles are lit. Teacher says: "Today we will each silently pray our own prayer, thinking it out instead of writing it. It may be a prayer of Adoration, of Confession, of Thanksgiving, or Supplication.

Step 7: <u>Teacher:</u> We conclude this study of prayer with two thoughts to remember. I have two small gifts to help you remember. (Give each child a sports card.) Keep this. Think about all the discipline that is involved in practicing a sport until you are really good at it. It is the same with playing the piano or any musical instrument. One musician said, "If I miss one day of practice I know it. If I miss two days of practice, the audience knows it. If I miss three days of practice, the whole world knows it." It is the same with prayer. We must constantly pray every day trying to be more open to God's voice speaking to us. Use this card to help you remember — Prayer takes practice.

Here is a second gift. (Give each child a sticker with a crown or some royal symbol.) This is to help you remember something else. Prayer is a privilege. Imagine you lived in a country with a king. Wouldn't it be wonderful if you were given the privilege of speaking to the king everyday? You are — in prayer.

Needed for Session Five:
1. pictures of Jesus praying in a variety of settings
2. large chart of portions of the Lord's Prayer
3. sports cards and royal emblem stickers

Session Five Outline:
1. Contest on pictures of Jesus praying.
2. Discussion.
3. Practice of Lord's Prayer.
4. Closing Time.